Happy ~~Birthday Kortnee~~!
I loo~~k~~ ~~forward to having a~~
drink ~~and~~ ~~cooking from this~~
book with you!
♡Emily

The Art of Vintage Cocktails

By Stephanie Rosenbaum ◆ Illustrations By Danielle Kroll

EGG&DART.PRESS

Copyright © 2013 by Dynamic Housewares Inc.

All rights reserved. No part of this book may be reproduced in any form without written permission from the publisher.

The advice recommendations and recipes may not be suitable for your situation. You should consult with a professional where appropriate. Neither the author nor the publisher shall be responsible or liable for any accident, injuries, losses, or other damages of any kind, including but not limited to personal, property, special, incidental, consequential or other damages.

ISBN 978-09887731-0-3

No use or depiction of any third party trade name, trademarks, service marks, or logos is intended to convey endorsement or other affiliation with this book. All such third party trade name, trademarks, service marks and logos are the property of their respective owners.

Manufactured in China

Designed by Danielle Kroll

10 9 8 7 6 5 4 3 2 1

First Edition

⬜EGG&DART.PRESS

www.egganddartpress.com

Table of Contents

INTRODUCTION

The Art of Vintage Cocktails

Behind every cocktail is a great story. It's not always the legendary one—those tall tales of invention are often too good to be true—but rather, the intriguing manner in which history, economics, chemistry, botany, geography, celebrity, exploration, and exploitation all come together, shaken or stirred into the magical elixirs we call cocktails.

Cocktails have been named after movie stars, Broadway shows, political victories, nightclubs, sporting events, and fads so fleeting that few can remember why or how they inspired a drink in the first place. Some cocktails demand the conviviality of a bar; others can be suavely shaken and sipped at home.

The Art of Vintage Cocktails welcomes you into the elegant world of the coupe, the flute, the rocks glass, and, of course, the perfect, iconically V-shaped martini glass. Some of the drinks you'll find in this spirited little tome are whimsical, long-lost creations due for a revival; others, like the daiquiri, have been so corrupted by cheap imitations that the appealing purity of their original proportions has been all but obscured. Let these pages take you back to a more stylish era, when gentlemen wore hats, ladies wore Arpège, and it was always five o'clock somewhere.

Our idea of vintage cocktail culture may be captured by silver-screen images of William Powell and Myrna Loy, but the most gorgeous flowering of the culture actually took place much earlier, during the Gilded Age of the mid to late 1800s through the twin upheavals of World War I and Prohibition. Mixologists like "Professor" Jerry Thomas, author of the first American cocktail guide in 1862, were stars at their trade, followed by regular customers whenever they switched saloons. One well-known New York City bartender claimed to invent a new drink every day. In high-end establishments, ingredients came from all around the world—French and German wines; liquors and liqueurs flavored with dozens or even hundreds of fruits, herbs, spices, and flowers—as well as from the bartender's own cabinet of housemade bitters, infusions, and syrups. The communal eighteenth-century punch bowl was slowly being replaced by the cocktail, a drink that was made *à la minute* as an experience for a singular drinker.

Nothing shaped cocktail culture as we know it more than the widespread adoption of the ice cube. Every bartender had his ice picks, planers, and scrapers to carve, shave, and crush ice in a wintery geometry of sizes and textures. Drinks could be poured over a cascade of diamond-clear cubes, or served up icy-cold, their surfaces frosted in a sheen of fragments.

The passage of the Eighteenth Amendment and the Volstead Act in 1920, which made it illegal to manufacture or sell intoxicating beverages, wiped away this elaborate cocktail culture. Cocktails—and drinking—continued, but in a very different form. Some nightclubs stayed open by simply selling "setups"—usually ice and soda water or ginger ale—that customers could then doctor to their tastes with their own spirituous supplies.

From the setup to the home bar wasn't much of a leap, since it was much safer to drink at home, as long as you weren't distilling the stuff in your backyard or bathtub. Following World War I, after the gains of the women's suffrage movement, drinking was no longer a men's game; at home or at the "speak," women were joining in the fun right alongside their male compan-

ions. Gin—or what passed for gin—reigned, and drinks were as fanciful as flapper's hats. Cuba, Puerto Rico, Mexico, London, Paris—wherever self-exiled drinkers flocked, they found bartenders willing to sell them the cocktails they craved. Rum, tequila, and even more exotic spirits like Brazilian cachaça became part of the American cocktail palate. When Prohibition ended in 1933, the time was ripe for a revival of public cocktail culture. Drinks could be elegant, witty, and carefully constructed again, and through the next few decades, the cocktail in all its many variations would be celebrated as one of the more enticing, delectable aspects of adult life.

With its whimsical mix of words and illustrations, *The Art of Vintage Cocktails* will inspire you to create your own good-spirited fun. With a little investment in a selection of quality spirits, liqueurs, and mixers, you can make the cocktail hour a time of personal expression, relaxation, and rejuvenation. From a classic Manhattan to a Prohibition-era Gin and Sin to a mid-century modern Vesper Martini, these delightful cocktails offer a chance to see through what inimitable writer (and peerless drinker) F. Scott Fitzgerald called the "rose-colored glasses of life." Cheers!

STOCKING YOUR VINTAGE BAR
Equipment and Ingredients

Vintage cocktails are made with fresh juices and fruits, pure sugar syrups, and an intriguing array of deliciously old-fashioned, once-obscure spirits and liqueurs, now happily easier to find in most well-stocked liquor stores.

SPIRITS AND LIQUEURS

Cachaça A fiery spirit made in Brazil from the first pressing of fresh sugarcane juice fermented in wood or copper casks.

Cocchi Apertivo Americano This Italian apertivo (similar to a dry vermouth) is the closest approximation of the original Kina Lillet.

Crème de Cassis A black currant liqueur, deep purple and fruity-tart, most typically mixed with white or sparkling wine make the French aperitifs known as Kir and Kir Royale.

Crème de Violette A purple infusion of violet petals and sugar in alcohol that smells and tastes like a bouquet of violets.

Drambuie Botanist and cocktail enthusiast Amy Stewart calls this a "rich and gorgeous liqueur made from Scotch, honey, saffron, nutmeg, and other mysterious spices."

Lillet A vermouth-like French aperitif, Lillet Blanc is made from white wine fortified with orange liqueur and flavored with botanicals, including cinchona bark. There's also red wine-based Lillet Rouge and a refreshing new Lillet Rosé.

Maraschino A lightly sweet, cherry-based liqueur with a hint of almond.

Pastis A family of anise-based spirits that turn milky or opalescent when water is added. Popular brands include Pernod, Ricard, Henri Bardouin, and in New Orleans, Herbsaint.

Pisco A clear spirit distilled from muscat wine. Look for Oro, Porton, and Campo de Encanto brands.

Sloe Gin The only sloe gin worth drinking is Plymouth Sloe Gin, imported from the U.K. and infused with real sloes, the black-skinned, bitter berry produced by the blackthorn bush.

Vermouth Both white and red vermouths are made from a white wine base fortified with grape brandy. Typically, white (French) vermouth is dry; red (Italian) vermouth is sweet.

MIXERS AND FLAVORINGS

Bitters Used just a drop at a time, these are intensely bitter, alcohol-based infusions made from aromatic herbs, barks, and spices. Artisanal companies now make bitters in flavors like rhubarb, blood orange, fig, even chocolate.

Cocktail Cherries It's time to dump the maraschino cherry for the grownup world of brandied cherries, marasca cherries, Italian amarena cherries, pickled cherries, and more.

Ginger Ale Look for brands made with pure cane sugar and real ginger root.

Ginger Beer Nonalcoholic ginger beer packs a hot, extra-gingery punch.

Grenadine Real grenadine syrup is made from sweetened pomegranate juice. Read the ingredient list before you buy; you're more likely to find real grenadine made by smaller artisanal local companies.

Gum (Gomme) Syrup A common ingredient in pre-Prohibition cocktail guides, gum syrup adds gum Arabic, the resin of the acacia tree, to simple syrup to produce a sweetening syrup with an extra-smooth mouthfeel.

Orgeat (pronounced or-ZHAT) A milky-looking almond syrup with a distinctively fragrant, bitter-almond flavor similar to marzipan or Amaretto.

Simple Syrup Mix 1 cup granulated sugar with 1 cup water. Heat, stirring frequently, until sugar is dissolved. Let cool, then cover and refrigerate.

EQUIPMENT

From Art Deco elegant to 50s kitschy, vintage (and vintage-style) barware exists to suit every taste. Besides shakers, pitchers, and glassware, you'll also need a few basic tools to make the cocktails in this book.

Jigger Shaped like two metal pyramids joined at the point, the jigger is the measuring cup of the bar. A large jigger measures $1\frac{1}{2}$ oz and $\frac{3}{4}$ oz; a small one, 1 oz and $\frac{1}{2}$ oz. In cocktail recipes, a jigger=$1\frac{1}{2}$ oz; a pony=1 oz.

Muddler Looks like a miniature wooden baseball bat. Used to crush or "muddle" fruits and/or herbs.

Shaker The typical shaker, also known as a Boston shaker, is a 3-part metal container, including a flared cylindrical cup, a strainer, and a cap.

Bar Spoon Long with a narrow twisted handle, it is useful to stir drinks or use to measure. 2 spoonfuls=$\frac{1}{4}$ ounce.

Strainer Look for a flat, oval strainer edged with a metal spring.

Glassware

Most vintage glassware is significantly smaller than today's jumbo-size drink vessels. Older, in this case, is smarter: smaller drinks stay fresh and properly chilled for just about the time it takes to drink them. If you're buying new glassware, look for smaller sizes, and avoid any martini glasses that could double as a burlesque dancer's bathtub.

Stemmed: *For drinks shaken or stirred and served up. The stem allows you to hold the glass while keeping the warmth of your hand away from your perfectly chilled cocktail.*

CHAMPAGNE COUPE

Also called a cocktail glass, this is a rounded, bowl-like stemmed glass, the kind you'd see in swanky party scenes in Hollywood movies from the 1930s and 1940s.

WINEGLASS

For wine-based cocktails, use a wineglass with a small bowl, like a white-wine glass. Save the goldfish-size bowls for your favorite red wine.

PORT GLASS

Small, short-stemmed wineglass, with a taller, narrower bowl.

CHAMPAGNE FLUTE

Tall, narrow stemmed glass, good for Champagne cocktails.

MARTINI GLASS

Shaped like an inverted pyramid, with the bowl ending in a point, this iconic shape dates from the 1925 Paris Art Deco exhibition.

Old fashioned: For drinks served over ice, especially those that are "built," or mixed together, right in the glass.

OLD FASHIONED (ROCKS)

Short, cylindrical glass with a heavy glass bottom.

DOUBLE OLD FASHIONED

Larger, wider cylindrical glass.

Highball: Used for long drinks, typically those served over ice with plenty of soda, tonic water, juice, or other mixers added.

HIGHBALL

Tall, straight, cylindrical glass, used for "long" drinks with ice and soda or mixers. Can also be used for juleps.

COLLINS

Narrower than a highball glass, usually the width of a single ice cube.

Others:

JULEP CUP

A tall metal cup that widens slightly toward the rim (like a pint glass); can be silver or pewter.

PUNCH GLASS

Small mug- or teacup-shaped glass with a handle, for hot or cold punches or toddies.

Glories
of the
GILDED
AGE

From Punch to Cocktails

During the late nineteenth century, few public establishments could beat a swanky big-city saloon for glamour, liveliness, and sheer entertainment value. Politicians and political fixers, opera singers and sportsmen, boulevardiers and bon vivants: they were the cast of a nightly show masterminded by a moustachioed master mixologist, his stage the bartop's acres of scrolled and polished mahogany, his footlights tiers of sparkling glassware shining by gaslight.

Equal parts showman, host, and artiste, this bartender dazzled his clientele with a well-shaken blend of charisma and chemistry. His swift-moving hands glittering with diamond rings, a diamond horseshoe anchoring his glossy tie, he turned the Gilded Age's ever-multiplying cocktail categories into fancifully named creations of his own. No longer did a customer ask for a simple sherry cobbler or gin fizz, or gather around a collective bowl of punch. Instead, he'd toast the day's good fortune with the Brain Duster or the Bijou, a Coronation or a Clover Club, all tricked out with fresh fruit, handmade syrups, high-quality liqueurs, wine, and spirits from around the world—and most importantly, ice, a suddenly affordable year-round luxury that set the shuffle of the cocktail shaker ringing up and down the boulevards.

This was the era that inspired many of the vintage cocktails still enjoyed today, from the Manhattan and the Mint Julep to the Sazerac and the Ramos Gin Fizz. So snap your sleeve garters, wax that moustache, and pull out the port, the pisco, and the pineapple. It's time to party like it's 1899!

Bijou

Think of an exquisitely wrought trinket, the sort with which a nineteenth-century Frenchman might adorn the powdered neck or scented wrist of his much-adored wife or *maîtresse*. Turn that trinket into a cocktail, and you've got the Bijou, a drink that derives its *je ne sais quoi* from three botanical spirits—gin, vermouth, and, most potently, green Chartreuse, an emerald green liqueur that's been made by Carthusian monks since 1764. The monks guard the secret formula for their liqueur religiously, but speculation suggests it includes mint, hyssop, lemon balm, angelica, anise, cardamom, wormwood, and up to one hundred other herbs, flowers, and spices.

1 ounce green Chartreuse
1 ounce sweet vermouth
1 ounce gin
Dash of orange bitters
Cocktail cherry and twist of lemon peel, for garnish

Combine Chartreuse, vermouth, gin, and bitters in a mixing glass with ice. Stir well. Strain into a chilled cocktail glass. Garnish with cherry and lemon twist.

Makes 1 drink

Black Velvet

This suavely brooding drink, made from three parts Champagne to two parts Guinness stout, was invented in 1861 by a bartender at the Brooks's Club in London. A dark drink suitable for mourning, it was made to honor Queen Victoria's beloved consort, the recently deceased Prince Albert.

The heavy, nearly black stout gives weight and gravitas to the Champagne. If you don't have a prince to toast (or a princely income), a decent dry sparkling wine will do just as well.

2 ounces chilled Guinness stout
3 ounces chilled Champagne or sparkling wine
Twist of lemon peel, for garnish

Pour Guinness into a chilled flute. Top with Champagne and garnish with lemon twist.

Makes 1 drink

Brain Duster

With its autumn leaf color and rye-and-vermouth base, this 1895 cocktail, born at the original Waldorf-Astoria hotel in New York, could easily pass for a Manhattan. But an ounce of absinthe makes the Brain Duster into an entirely different—and much more lethal—drink.

Still, the Green Fairy, as absinthe is known, can be an acquired taste. You could also toast auld lang syne with a Bobby Burns cocktail, named after Scotland's best-loved poet: replace the rye and absinthe with two ounces of good blended Scotch and add a few dashes of Drambuie, a whiskey-based liqueur flavored with herbs and heather honey. Leave in the bitters to balance the Drambuie's hint of sweetness.

1 ounce rye whiskey

1 ounce absinthe

1 ounce sweet vermouth

Dash of Angostura bitters

Twist of lemon peel, for garnish

Combine rye, absinthe, vermouth, and bitters in a mixing glass with ice. Stir well. Strain into a chilled cocktail glass. Garnish with lemon twist.

Makes 1 drink

Bronx

Of the five boroughs of New York City, only Manhattan and the Bronx have found lasting fame at the bar. Like its namesake, the glamorous Manhattan (page 32) has long overshadowed its sister cocktail, the Bronx, but it wasn't always that way. Invented at the bar of the posh Waldorf-Astoria hotel, the Bronx (named for the zoo) was one of the hotel's most popular drinks during pre-Prohibition years.

1 ounce gin

1 ounce orange juice, preferably freshly squeezed

½ ounce dry vermouth

½ ounce sweet vermouth

Orange slice, for garnish

Combine gin, orange juice, and vermouths in a shaker with ice. Shake well. Strain into a chilled cocktail glass and garnish with the orange slice.

Makes 1 drink

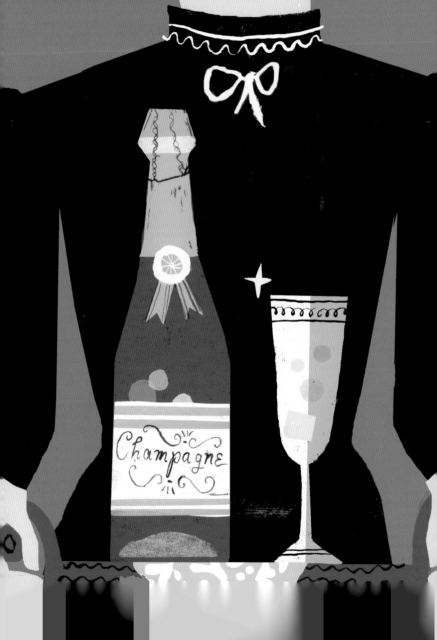

Champagne Cocktail

A touch of bitters, a bit of sugar, and a nip of cognac: they're the string of pearls against Champagne's little black dress, elevating an already glamorous drink to the epitome of elegance in a glass—appropriate, given its history as the favored libation of Parisian courtesans during the Belle Époque. If you can find brown (Demerara) sugar cubes, try them; they add a little more depth and toasty flavor than regular white sugar.

6 or 7 drops Angostura bitters

1 sugar cube, brown or white

Splash of cognac

Chilled Champagne

Twist of orange or lemon peel, for garnish (optional)

Drip bitters onto sugar cube to saturate. Drop the bitters-soaked cube into the bottom of a chilled flute. Add just enough cognac to cover the sugar. Pour in Champagne to fill slowly, as it will foam up when it touches the sugar. Once it stops foaming, garnish with orange or lemon twist, if desired.

Makes 1 drink

Clover Club

You could call the Clover Club the Cosmo of its day: pink, pretty, and downed by the dozen by bons vivants and sporting gents who propped up the bars of Philadelphia, New York, Baltimore, and beyond. The Clover Club was the house drink of a men's club by the same name, known to meet at the bar of Philadelphia's Bellevue-Stratford hotel for some three decades between the 1880s and World War I.

As in other popular turn-of-the-century drinks—such as the Pisco Sour, the Pink Lady, the Ramos Gin Fizz—egg whites are a key ingredient, giving the drink smoothness, body, and a distinctive frothy head. One egg white should be enough for at least two drinks; a brief whisking will loosen the white enough to divide.

2 ounces gin

1 ounce freshly squeezed lemon juice

½ teaspoon superfine sugar

½ egg white

2 teaspoons grenadine, or to taste

Lemon slice, for garnish

Combine gin, lemon juice, sugar, egg white, and grenadine in a shaker with cracked ice. Shake vigorously to emulsify the egg white thoroughly. Strain into a chilled goblet or cocktail glass. Garnish with lemon slice.

Makes 1 drink

Coronation

Edward VII, crowned in 1901, launched the Edwardian era, a brief but charming period that lives in memory as a perpetual summer lawn party of cricket, cucumber sandwiches, starched white linen, and Champagne. One of several variations, all named for Edward's coronation, this Coronation uses dry sherry as the base, making it a lovely, lighter warm-weather drink.

The writer Henry James, himself a lifelong Anglophile, once said that the two most beautiful words in the English language were *summer afternoon*, and with one of these in hand, you'll certainly agree.

Long, thin spiral of orange peel, for garnish

1½ ounces fino sherry

1½ ounces dry vermouth

¼ ounce Luxardo maraschino

2 dashes of orange bitters

Wrap orange peel around the handle of a wooden spoon to curl. Combine sherry, vermouth, maraschino, and bitters in a mixing glass with ice. Stir well. Strain into a chilled cocktail glass. Slide curled peel into the drink to garnish.

Makes 1 drink

Corpse Reviver #2

Gin and absinthe: Not just for breakfast anymore! The Corpse Reviver isn't simply one cocktail; in the pre-Prohibition era, Corpse Revivers were a whole category of back-from-the-dead eye-openers, morning drinks made to revive even the most hungover imbiber. Out of a long numbered list, #2 has survived to find a place again on contemporary cocktail menus.

If you don't have absinthe on hand, use a dash of pastis, such as Pernod or Ricard. And watch out—as famed barman Harry Craddock once said, "Four of these taken in swift succession will unrevive the corpse again."

¾ ounce gin

¾ ounce Cointreau

¾ ounce Lillet Blanc or Cocchi Aperitivo Americano

¾ ounce freshly squeezed lemon juice

A few drops of absinthe*

Combine ingredients in a shaker with ice. Shake well. Strain into a chilled cocktail glass.

You can also rinse the glass with absinthe rather than mixing it into the drink.

Makes 1 drink

Enchantress

This rich garnet drink hails from San Francisco, where it was recorded in 1867 by bartender Charles B. Campbell in his post–Gold Rush cocktail guide. Where he got the name, no one knows, but one can easily imagine a Gilded Age gentleman, built along the lines of industrialist Leland Stanford or railroad magnate Charles Crocker, entertaining a gorgeously attired and lushly bejeweled opera singer in a candle-lit hideaway draped with velvet curtains. What better drink to charm such a creature with than a ruby-colored Enchantress?

2 ounces ruby port

2 ounces brandy

½ ounce orange curaçao, or to taste

½ ounce freshly squeezed lemon juice

Combine ingredients in a shaker with crushed ice. Shake well. Pour the drink with a handful of ice into a wineglass and serve with a straw. To serve up, strain into a chilled wineglass or cocktail glass.

Makes 1 drink

Fish House Punch

Redolent of rum, brandy, and peaches, this rambunctious party drink dates back to the eighteenth century, an era of grand imbibing where every celebration called for rounds of toasts around a communal bowl of punch. This particular punch was the house specialty of a rustic rod-and-gun club near Philadelphia known as the State in Schuylkill, whose founding predated the Declaration of Independence by some forty-four years.

Peels from 3 lemons

2¼ cups raw or Demerara sugar (light brown sugar can be substituted for a sweeter punch)

3 quarts water

2 cups freshly squeezed lemon juice

3½ cups cognac or brandy

2¼ cups dark rum

3 ounces good-quality peach brandy, such as Marie Brizard

Large block or mold of ice, for serving

In a large heatproof mixing bowl, muddle lemon peels with sugar. (This releases the peels' aromatic oil so the sugar can absorb it.) Heat 2 cups of the water to boiling, and then pour over the sugar and stir until dissolved. Add lemon juice, Cognac, rum, peach brandy, and remaining cold water. Remove lemon peels. Chill for several hours. To serve, pour into a large punch bowl and add ice block or mold. Ladle into individual cups.

Makes 10 to 12 servings

Manhattan

Like the martini, the Manhattan seems like the quintessential 1950s cocktail. Surprisingly, this combination of rye whisky, sweet vermouth, and bitters dates back to the 1880s, when vermouth was just coming into vogue as an aperitif and cocktail ingredient. In fact, the popularity of both the Manhattan and the Martini did much to establish vermouth's place as an essential ingredient of the mixologist's art.

A Perfect Manhattan is made with equal parts sweet and dry vermouth, while a Dry Manhattan substitutes French (dry) vermouth and is garnished with a lemon twist. Like many drinks made only with spirits, it should be stirred, not shaken, to preserve the clarity of the drink.

2 ounces rye whiskey

½ ounce sweet vermouth

1 or 2 dashes Angostura bitters (orange bitters may be substituted)

Cocktail cherry, for garnish

Combine rye, vermouth, and bitters in a mixing glass with ice. Stir well. Strain into a chilled cocktail glass. Garnish with cherry.

Makes 1 drink

I LIKE *to* HAVE A MARTINI

Two AT THE VERY most

AFTER THREE *I'm under The Table*

AFTER FOUR
I'M UNDER
my host

– DOROTHY PARKER

Martinez

Old Tom gin, a remnant of the Gilded Age, doesn't look or taste anything like today's style of gin. Instead of the clear, juniper-piney bite of London dry gin, Old Tom looks like whiskey and tastes like it, too, with a sweet, malty edge and softer botanicals. This makes the West Coast–born Martinez a bridge between the rye whiskey–based Manhattan and the classic gin-based martini.

While Martini lovers may pride themselves on using as little vermouth as possible (how dry can you go?), the Martinez harks back to an earlier, more vermouth-friendly era, using twice as much vermouth as gin, plus a hint of maraschino and a dash of bitters. This makes it a cocktail worth sipping, without the risks enumerated by poet-satirist Dorothy Parker: "I like to have a martini, / Two at the very most. / After three I'm under the table, / After four I'm under my host."

1 ounce Old Tom gin

2 ounces sweet vermouth

1 teaspoon Luxardo maraschino

Dash of bitters

Combine gin, vermouth, maraschino, and bitters in a mixing glass with ice. Stir well. Strain into a chilled cocktail glass.

Makes 1 drink

Mint Julep

Who can watch the Kentucky Derby, the most famous of America's horse races, without a mint julep in hand? Start with Kentucky bourbon, pour over plenty of ice in a frosted silver julep cup, and cool down with a sprig of fresh mint and a bit of fizz.

According to what we've heard, a true Southern lady never asks for another round of juleps. Instead, she just accepts a little "freshening" of her glass with a drop (or two or three) of bourbon to help that minty sugar water down.

12 fresh mint leaves

½ ounce simple syrup (page 7), or to taste

2 ounces bourbon whiskey

Chilled soda water (optional)

Long sprig of fresh mint, for garnish

Fill a tall, chilled glass or metal julep cup with crushed ice and stir vigorously until the glass is frosted. Discard ice. Add mint leaves and simple syrup and muddle gently. Pour in bourbon. Fill glass with crushed ice and stir well. If desired, top up with soda water. Garnish with mint sprig.

Makes 1 drink

Pisco Sour

San Francisco after the Gold Rush was a lively, boisterous, yet cosmopolitan place, a crossroads between East and West. Everything and everyone arrived on the shores of the Barbary Coast, and one of the city's favorite spirits was Pisco, a fiery Peruvian brandy distilled from wine made from muscat grapes planted by Spanish colonists.

En route around Cape Horn, westbound ships would put into the Peruvian port town of Pisco to resupply, picking up a stock of the local brandy for lucrative resale among the thirsty saloons up north. From grand hotels to waterfront dives, San Franciscans kept the fog at bay with potent Pisco Sours, a favorite of two writers about town: Jack London and Mark Twain.

2 ounces pisco

¾ ounce simple syrup (page 7), or to taste

¾ ounce freshly squeezed lemon juice, or a combination of lemon and lime juice

1 egg white

A few drops of orange bitters, for garnish

Combine pisco, simple syrup, lemon juice, and egg white in a shaker. Dry shake to emulsify. Add a handful of ice and shake vigorously until drink is smooth and foamy. Strain into a chilled old fashioned glass. Shake a few drops of bitters on top.

Makes 1 drink

Prince of Wales

Queen Victoria's son Edward, Prince of Wales, didn't ascend to the throne until 1901, when he was sixty years old. That left plenty of time for playing the ponies, pursuing pretty women, and downing enough Champagne to refloat the *Titanic*. When he wasn't knocking back the bubbly, he was enjoying a good cocktail (or four), often topped up with Champagne.

According to *The Private Life of King Edward VII*, a tell-all memoir published by "A Member of the Royal Household" in 1901, this fruity but powerful concoction was one of Edward's favorites.

1 teaspoon superfine sugar
Dash of Angostura or orange bitters
½ teaspoon water
1½ ounces rye whiskey
Splash of maraschino liqueur
1 chunk fresh (or canned in juice) pineapple
1 ounce chilled Champagne
Twist of lemon peel, for garnish

Put sugar, bitters, and ½ teaspoon water in a shaker. Using a bar spoon, stir until sugar is dissolved. Add rye, maraschino, pineapple chunk, and a handful of cracked ice. Shake vigorously to crush the pineapple. Strain into a chilled cocktail glass and top with Champagne. Garnish with lemon twist.

Makes 1 drink

Ramos Gin Fizz

Invented in New Orleans by bar owner Henry Ramos in 1888, this eye-opener is one of the great brunch drinks. The trick to getting the texture right—part velvet, part fizz—is in the shaking. Ramos was known for employing a line of a dozen or more "shaker boys" behind his bars to shake and pass every fizz ordered from hand to hand down the line.

A good, hard shaking is necessary to thicken the egg and cream and turn the whole concoction into a fragrant, go-down-easy delight. But if you don't have a line of Big Easy shaker boys waiting to do your bidding, whizzing the mixture in a blender with a handful of crushed ice for about 20 seconds works, too.

1½ ounces gin

½ ounce freshly squeezed lemon juice

½ ounce freshly squeezed lime juice

1 to 1½ teaspoons simple syrup (page 7), to taste

2 ounces heavy cream

1 small egg white, or ½ large or
extra-large egg white

3 or 4 drops orange flower water

Chilled club soda or soda water

Combine gin, lemon and lime juice, simple syrup, cream, egg white, and orange flower water in a shaker with ice. Shake vigorously for several minutes. Strain into a chilled highball or wineglass. Top with soda.

Makes 1 drink

Rum Daisy

The Daisy is rarely seen on today's bar menus, but back in the late decades of the nineteenth century, rum, gin, and whiskey daisies kept good company with the refreshing fizzes and sours that were replacing the elaborate cobblers, flips, and punches of an earlier era.

According to cocktail historian David Wondrich, the Daisy may even be the precursor to the margarita, as Mexican and Southwestern bartenders replaced rum with tequila and swapped lime juice for lemon. (*Margarita* is, after all, the Spanish word for "daisy".) The original is still an enchanting little drink, rosy with grenadine or scented with Grand Marnier. You can also make a deliciously summery raspberry daisy by substituting raspberry syrup for the grenadine.

2 ounces dark rum

Juice of ½ lemon

½ teaspoon superfine sugar, or to taste

1 teaspoon grenadine or 1½ teaspoons Grand Marnier or curaçao

Chilled soda water (optional)

Combine rum, lemon juice, sugar, and grenadine in a shaker with ice. Strain into a chilled cocktail glass if serving up. For a longer drink, strain into a chilled old fashioned glass, add ice, and top with a few squirts of soda water.

Makes 1 drink

Sazerac

This 1800s New Orleans classic has its roots in the bitters invented by Antoine Peychaud, a pharmacist from Santo Domingo who settled in the Crescent City. He touted Peychaud's Bitters as a digestif and all-around cure-all, especially when added to a glass of cognac.

Over the years, this early version of the cocktail followed fashion as the cognac was replaced with rye whiskey and a splash of absinthe—with its distinctive licorice taste and high-proof herbal/wormwood kick—was added. After absinthe was outlawed in 1912 it was replaced by Herbsaint, a less potent pastis.

Splash of absinthe, Herbsaint, or Pernod

1 teaspoon sugar

1 teaspoon water

2 ounces rye whiskey

3 or 4 dashes Peychaud's bitters

Twist of lemon peel, for garnish

Rinse the inside of a chilled old fashioned glass with absinthe, Herbsaint, or Pernod, pouring out any excess liquid. Stir sugar with 1 teaspoon water in glass until dissolved. In a mixing glass, combine rye, bitters, and ice cubes together to chill. Strain into absinthe-rinsed glass. Garnish with lemon twist.

Makes 1 drink

Weeper's Joy

Cocktail historian David Wondrich said that the legendary New York City mixologist William Schmidt claimed to invent a new cocktail every day. To preserve his inventions for posterity, the formidably mustachioed Schmidt penned *The Flowing Bowl: When and What to Drink*, a how-to for many of his most famous inventions.

This one, the Weeper's Joy, showcases the sweet, caraway-scented spirit called kummel, originally Dutch but now also made in Germany, Russia, and Scandinavia. Like the Bijou (page 13), this is a complex drink, thanks to the many-layered botanicals found in the absinthe, vermouth, and kummel, whose flavorings also include pungent cumin and anise-y fennel. It is a reward for the bold of palate, who may well weep with joy when presented with this very grown-up drink.

1 ounce absinthe

1 ounce high-quality sweet vermouth, such as Carpano Antica

1 ounce kummel

½ teaspoon simple syrup (page 7)

2 dashes of curaçao

Combine ingredients in a mixing glass with ice. Stir well. Strain into a chilled cocktail glass.

Makes 1 drink

ROARING Twenties -AND- Prohibition

Bootleg Whiskey
and Bathtub Gin

Thank the Eighteenth Amendment, which prohibited the manufacture and sale of intoxicating liquors, for the stylish bar cabinet in your living room. Before Prohibition came into effect in 1920, drinking was most typically done outside the home, whether at a swanky hotel bar or a humble, sawdust-floored saloon where the beer was cheap and the lunch was free. Once the Volstead Act came into effect to enforce the law, mixing cocktails at home suddenly made a lot more sense. How you came by your spirits was your own affair, but department stores were more than happy to sell elegant barware for the home, complete with shakers, strainers, ice buckets, and cocktail glasses in all shapes and sizes. Prohibition didn't kill cocktail culture—it just sent it underground, sometimes literally, into a network of speakeasies and back-alley joints. With women joining in the fun, girlier drinks like the Brandy Alexander, the Gin and Sin, and the Bee's Knees rose to meet flapper demand and were emphatically enjoyed by both sexes.

Travel across the border became particularly appealing during Prohibition, and the manufacturers of Mexican tequila and Cuban rum were happy to lure American tourists with the promise of free-flowing cocktails like the Nationale, El Presidente, and the Hemingway Daiquiri. Returning home, Americans brought a taste for these spirits, and the tropical cocktails made with them, back to their living-room bars. Prohibition may have ended the grand era of the showman bartender, but it created a new generation of home mixologists, eager to show off their skills once the shades were drawn against any prying temperance-minded neighbors.

Agua Caliente

In 1920, as soon as Texas went dry, thrill seekers flocked to Tijuana's Agua Caliente racetrack, where they could play the ponies and enjoy fanciful drinks like the original Tequila Sunrise, whose flaming color came from a combination of gold tequila, purple crème de cassis, and pink grenadine.

Sadly, back across the border, fancy French liqueurs were in short supply. The Tequila Sunrise lost its elegant reputation and became known only for being garishly colored, strong, and a little trashy. So, we've renamed the original recipe after its Mexican birthplace, Agua Caliente. Given the well-known kick of tequila, one too many of these might very well find you in agua caliente ("hot water") indeed.

¾ ounce simple syrup (page 7), or to taste

1½ ounces freshly squeezed lime juice

1½ ounces tequila

2 ounces club soda or sparkling water

½ ounce crème de cassis

2 dashes of grenadine

In a tall highball glass, combine simple syrup and lime juice. Fill glass with ice and stir. Add tequila, followed by club soda. Slowly pour the cassis down the center of the glass, followed by the grenadine, and serve without stirring.

Makes 1 drink

Aviation

What's the cocktail forecast? Cool and clear, perfect for a tart and racy trip above the clouds with this high-flying blend of gin, lemon, maraschino liqueur, and crème de violette, a deliciously recherché floral liqueur. Impossible to find for decades, this violet-tinged retro delight was recently reintroduced by distillers Rothman & Winter in a sleek Deco bottle that makes a very stylish addition to any vintage-themed drinks cabinet. While you can make an Aviation without it, only a dash of crème de violette can give this cocktail its perfect twilight-above-the-clouds hue.

If you order the Aviation at a bar, make sure the mixologist on duty has a bottle of Luxardo maraschino on hand; trying to substitute the runoff from a bottle of maraschino cherries will send your drink into a sticky tailspin crash.

1½ ounces gin
½ ounce Luxardo maraschino
½ ounce crème de violette (optional)
½ ounce freshly squeezed lemon juice, or to taste
Cocktail cherry, for garnish

Combine gin, maraschino, crème de violette (if using), and lemon juice with ice in a shaker. Shake well. Strain into a chilled cocktail or martini glass. Garnish with cherry.

Makes 1 drink

Bee's Knees

The Bright Young Things of the 1920s were mad for all kinds of fads, crazes, and slang. The bee's knees, the cat's pajamas: these were the kind of nonsense phrases that became part of what newspapers of the time sarcastically called the "Flapper's Dictionary." It didn't take long for an enterprising bartender to whip up a honey-based gin cocktail and dub it the Bee's Knees.

If you're planning on serving a party's worth of Bee's Knees, you might want to mix up some honey syrup. An easy-to-make version of simple syrup (page 7), it blends much more easily than regular honey. Use equal parts water and a mild-flavored honey, like clover or wildflower. Warm the water on the stove until it's hot but not boiling. Stir in the honey until dissolved. Let cool and refrigerate until needed. Start with ½ ounce (1 tablespoon) of honey syrup per drink, adding more to taste.

2 ounces gin

½ ounce freshly squeezed lemon or lime juice

1 teaspoon honey or 1 tablespoon honey syrup (see recipe, introduction),
or to taste

Lemon or lime slice, for garnish

Combine ingredients in a shaker with cracked ice. Shake well. Strain into a chilled cocktail glass. Garnish with lemon wheel.

Makes 1 drink

Between the Sheets

Harry MacElhone of the storied Harry's at the Ritz in Paris probably shook up the first Between the Sheets in the 1920s. Calling for brandy, rum, and Cointreau, this naughtily named but elegantly slinky drink could most certainly send you sliding between the (satin) sheets with whatever lovely you've been romancing at the bar.

You can also try out the version created by "King Cocktail" Dale DeGroff: three parts cognac, two parts lemon juice, and one part each Benedictine and Cointreau. Flaming the orange peel—another DeGroff suggestion—adds a nice touch of drama to the presentation.

¾ ounce cognac or brandy

¾ ounce dark rum

¾ ounce Cointreau

¾ ounce freshly squeezed lemon juice

Flamed orange peel or twist of orange peel, for garnish

Combine ingredients in a shaker with ice and shake well. Strain into a chilled cocktail glass. To flame orange peel, hold a wide strip of orange peel by its ends between your thumb and forefinger, orange side down. Hold a lit match below the peel. Squeeze your thumb and forefinger together and "snap" the peel to release its oils over the match. Drop peel into drink after flaming, or simply garnish with orange twist.

Makes 1 drink

"At The George Bar He ordered 'Four Alexander Cocktails, please,' 'ranged them Before Them With a Loud 'YUM YUM' Which drew every Eye, Outraged, Upon him 'I Expect you Prefer Sherry but, MY DEAR CHARLES, you're NOT going To have Sherry. Isn't THIS A DELICIOUS CONCOCTION? you don't like it? Then I will Drink it for you. 1, 2, 3, 4, DOWN THE RED LANE THEY GO. HOW STUDENTS STARE!'" —ANTHONY BLANCHE in Evelyn Waugh's novel BRIDESHEAD REVISITED

Brandy Alexander

"I expect you prefer sherry but, my dear Charles, you're not going to *have* sherry. Isn't this a delicious concoction? You don't like it? Then I will drink it for you. One, two, three, four, down the red lane they go. *How* the students stare!"

So says the self-consciously louche Anthony Blanche in Evelyn Waugh's novel *Brideshead Revisited*, set in 1923. But just what is this delicious concoction—a drink or a dessert? And was it named for Russian Tsar Alexander II, or sharp-tongued Algonquin Round Table writer Alexander Woollcott?

Replace the brandy with crème de menthe, and you'll have a Grasshopper, the Alexander's minty cousin. But unless you're a very naughty (and fictional) character, we'd never suggest drinking four of these, as Blanche does, before dinner.

½ ounce brandy

½ ounce crème de cacao

½ ounce half-and-half

Freshly grated nutmeg, for garnish (optional)

Combine ingredients in a shaker with ice. Shake well. Strain into a chilled cocktail glass or brandy snifter. Add a dusting of nutmeg over the surface, if desired.

Makes 1 drink

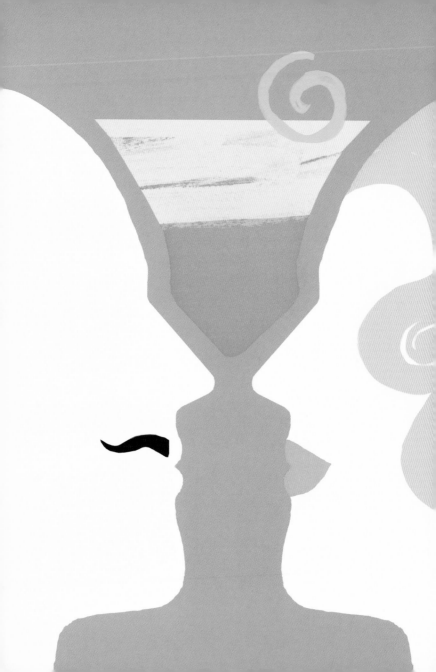

Douglas Fairbanks

Before the advent of the "talkies," movie star Douglas Fairbanks (1883–1939) epitomized all that was madly dashing and handsome in silent films. He played swashbuckling pirates and alluring rogues who always got the girl, starring in *The Mark of Zorro* (the blockbuster of its time), *Robin Hood*, *The Three Musketeers*, and dozens of others.

Cocktail legend has it that when Fairbanks found out that his wife, the much-adored Hollywood actress Mary Pickford, had a namesake cocktail, he challenged a Havana bartender to make one of his own. Who would say no to a man dubbed "The King of Hollywood"? This racy, apricot-hued delight is the result.

1½ ounces gin

1 ounce apricot brandy

½ ounce freshly squeezed lime juice

Twist of lemon peel, for garnish

Combine ingredients in a shaker with ice. Shake well. Strain into a chilled cocktail glass. Garnish with lemon twist.

Makes 1 drink

El Presidente

Like the Bacardi cocktail (rum, lime juice, and grenadine) and the Daiquiri, the glowing, ruby-red El Presidente was one of the great rum classics enjoyed by Prohibition-era American visitors to Havana's beautiful beaches and anything-goes nightclubs. It was named in honor of Mario García Menocal, Cuba's president from 1913 to 1921.

While the ingredients and the rum base remain constant, the proportions for this drink can vary according to the bartender; some use twice as much Cointreau as vermouth, others the reverse. This classic version is made with equal parts rum and Dolin Vermouth Blanc, a semi-dry French vermouth whose sweetness smoothes out the rum without being cloying.

1½ ounces Cuban light rum
1½ ounces Dolin Vermouth Blanc
½ ounce Cointreau or curaçao
Dash of grenadine

Combine rum, vermouth, Cointreau, and grenadine in a shaker with ice. Shake well. Strain into a chilled cocktail glass.

Makes 1 drink

Gin and Sin

Does any other cocktail name capture the gin-loving, rum-running, speakeasy era of 1920s Prohibition as perfectly as the Gin and Sin? We can imagine would-be starlets, fresh off the Super Chief train from Chicago, getting wooed by producers in a Hollywood hideaway. With Los Angeles still a land of orange groves, what better introduction to the golden West than a Gin and Sin, made where oranges grew on trees right in front of your bungalow, and any platinum-haired sweetheart was just a screen test away from stardom?

1½ ounces gin

1 ounce freshly squeezed orange juice

1 ounce freshly squeezed lemon juice

½ teaspoon grenadine

Twisted orange slice, for garnish

Combine ingredients in a shaker with cracked ice. Shake well. Strain into a chilled cocktail glass or serve on the rocks in an old fashioned glass. Garnish with twisted orange slice.

Makes 1 drink

Hemingway Daiquiri

As soon as Prohibition was declared, Havana began marketing itself as a tropical getaway for Americans longing for sun, fun, and rum. Bacardi salesmen handed Bacardi cocktails to debarking passengers right in the airport.

The daiquiri, was nothing more than two parts light rum, one part freshly squeezed lime juice, and a dash of simple syrup. But at the Bar La Floridain Havana, Ernest Hemingway's favorite version of this drink became a draw unto itself—especially when "Papa" was knocking back a few at his favorite spot at the end of the bar.

1½ ounces Cuban light rum

Juice of 1 lime

Splash of freshly squeezed grapefruit juice

Splash of Luxardo maraschino

1 teaspoon simple syrup (page 7), or to taste

Lime slice, for garnish

Combine rum, lime juice, grapefruit juice, maraschino, and simple syrup in a shaker with cracked ice. Shake well. Strain into a chilled cocktail glass. Garnish with lime slice.

Note: Papa drank his daiquiris without sugar; try one without the syrup if you like your drinks on the sour side.

Makes 1 drink

Maiden's Prayer

In *Cocktail: The Drinks Bible for the 21st Century*, authors Laura Moorhead and "The Alchemist" Paul Harrington insist that this speakeasy staple is best made using California's sweet, fragrant Meyer lemons. Not surprisingly, Harrington made his name as a classic-cocktail revivalist behind the bar at the once venerable Enrico's in North Beach, a longtime hangout for San Francisco's Beats and bohemians.

If you're lucky enough to find yourself in San Francisco on a sunny afternoon just before the fog rolls in, pick a lemon or two (plus a few of its gorgeously scented blossoms), shake up a round for your friends, and offer up a Maiden's Prayer for your good fortune.

¾ ounce gin

¾ ounce light rum

¾ ounce Cointreau

½ ounce freshly squeezed lemon juice, preferably from Meyer lemons

Twist of lemon peel or fresh lemon blossom, for garnish

Combine ingredients in a shaker with crushed ice. Shake well. Strain into a chilled cocktail glass. Garnish with lemon peel or lemon blossom.

Makes 1 drink

Nationale

Lesser known nowadays than some of the other rum drinks and punches popularized by Prohibition-era visitors to Cuba's splashy bars and nightclubs, this golden drink, named for the Hotel Nationale in Havana, is a lushly fruity sundowner that balances the sweetness of rum and apricot brandy with a generous splash of lime juice and a dash of peach bitters.

It's perfect for enjoying beachside as the sun drops into the ocean at the end of another perfect summer day. Need to warm your spirits even on a snowy day? Put on a good Cuban mambo, crack open the rum, and bring summer back with a round of Nationales.

1½ ounces golden rum

¾ ounce apricot brandy, such as Marie Brizard Apry

1 ounce freshly squeezed lime juice

¾ ounce pineapple syrup or simple syrup (page 7)

A couple dashes of peach bitters

Lime slice, for garnish

Combine rum, brandy, lime juice, pineapple syrup, and bitters in a shaker with ice. Shake well. Strain into a chilled coupe. Garnish with lime slice.

Makes 1 drink

Negroni

People who like Negronis like them very, very much. Cocktail legend has it that the Negroni was named for Florentine aristocrat Count Camillo Negroni, who juiced up the then-popular Americano (Campari, sweet vermouth, and soda water) with a shot of gin back in the 1920s. Campari's bitter bite can take some getting used to, but once you're hooked, you'll find this astringent, appetite-whetting *aperitivo* keeps palates fresh and dinner conversation keen.

Want to go one modern step beyond the Negroni? Bump up to 1¾ ounces Carpano Punt e Mes (a dry vermouth) mixed with 1¾ ounces Hendrick's gin, and then stir in the usual ounce of Campari. I Sodi, a restaurant in New York City, calls this the Punt-e-Groni, and cocktail writer Jonathan Miles describes it as "so gorgeously bitter...[d]rinking it is like being slapped by an ex-lover."

1 ounce gin
1 ounce sweet vermouth, such as Noilly Prat or Carpano Antica
1 ounce Campari
Half-slice of orange, for garnish

Combine gin, vermouth, and Campari in a mixing glass with ice. Stir well. Strain into a chilled old fashioned glass over ice or serve up in a chilled cocktail glass. Squeeze orange half-slice gently into the drink and then drop in.

Makes 1 drink

Satan's Whiskers

Perhaps it was the gin that gave this cocktail, invented in Hollywood in 1930, its diabolical edge. During Prohibition, gin had a racy reputation and a not-so-pure history. What was sold as gin during that time wasn't the reliable, juniper-scented spirit of a summer's worth of gin and tonics; often, "gin" was anything that could be distilled, its rough-and-ready nature hidden under a cloak of sugar and fake botanical flavorings.

But made well, this is a drink worthy of a high-class speakeasy, built with French Grand Marnier, fresh orange juice, and both French dry and Italian sweet vermouth. If you prefer your whiskers "curled" instead of "straight," replace the Grand Mariner with curaçao.

1 ounce gin

½ ounce dry vermouth

½ ounce sweet vermouth

½ ounce Grand Marnier

1 ounce freshly squeezed orange juice

Dash of orange bitters

Orange slice, for garnish

Combine ingredients in a shaker with cracked ice. Shake well. Strain into a chilled cocktail glass. Garnish with orange slice.

Makes 1 drink

Scofflaw

While temperance was the law during the thirteen years of Prohibition between 1920 and 1933, there was no shortage of risk-taking drinkers, distillers, and distributors willing to flout the rules. Disdain for the Eighteenth Amendment was so widespread that in 1924, the *Boston Herald* ran a $200 contest to coin a new word for those criminals who refused to let the party end.

Scofflaw was the winner, and shortly thereafter, Harry's New York Bar in Paris (where, of course, it was still legal to drink) created the Scofflaw, an instant hit among its expat clientele.

1½ ounces rye or blended whiskey

1 ounce dry vermouth

½ ounce freshly squeezed lemon juice

Dash of orange bitters

½ ounce grenadine (optional)

Lemon slice, for garnish

Combine whiskey, vermouth, lemon juice, and bitters in a shaker with cracked ice. Shake well. Strain into a chilled cocktail glass. Drizzle in grenadine, if using, without stirring. Garnish with lemon slice.

Makes 1 drink

The Boston Herald

SCOFFLAW!

Sidecar

One should save the Sidecar for a classy hotel bar. As Raymond Chandler writes in his classic noir *The Long Goodbye*, "I like bars just after they open for the evening . . . I like to watch the man mix the first one of the evening and put it down on a crisp mat and put the little folded napkin beside it. I like to taste it slowly. The first quiet drink of the evening in a quiet bar—that's wonderful."

The Sidecar is a silk-stocking taste of the lush life in 1920s Paris where, as society chronicler Basil Woon wrote, "skirts were short, francs were cheap."

Granulated sugar, for frosting glass

Orange or lemon slice, for frosting glass

2 ounces cognac

½ ounce Cointreau

½ ounce freshly squeezed lemon juice

Twist of orange or lemon peel, for garnish

To frost glass: Spread sugar across a small plate or saucer. Swipe the outer rim of the glass with orange or lemon slice. Twist the wet edge of the glass in the sugar to make an even ribbon of sugar around the outside of the glass. Tap off excess. Let set until firm and dry and then chill glasses as needed in the freezer.

Combine cognac, Cointreau, and lemon juice in a shaker with ice. Shake well. Strain into frosted, chilled cocktail glass. Garnish with orange peel.

Makes 1 drink

Singapore Sling

Created around 1915 by Ngiam Tong Boon, a bartender at the swanky Long Bar of the Raffles Hotel in Singapore, the Singapore Sling is a long drink, made with the gin preferred by its expat English clientele and refreshed with plenty of ice and club soda.

Made to work its magic even on the most monsoon-muggy of nights, simpler versions do the trick with just gin, cherry brandy, lemon juice, and a dash of simple syrup (page 7). But the version offered here is closer to the more baroque original, complete with Cointreau and Benedictine. If you really want to go for baroque, cut back on the soda water and add a few ounces of pineapple juice.

1½ ounces gin

½ ounce cherry brandy, such as Cherry Heering

½ ounce freshly squeezed lime juice

2 dashes of Cointreau

2 dashes of Benedictine (authentic, but optional)

Dash of Angostura bitters

Soda water

Cocktail cherry and orange slice, for garnish

Half fill a highball glass with ice. Combine gin, cherry brandy, lime juice, Cointreau, Benedictine, and bitters in a shaker with ice. Shake well. Strain into highball glass and top off with soda water. Garnish with cherry and orange slice.

Makes 1 drink

Stinger

Where's the sting in this drink? In the minty bite of the crème de menthe, of course! This short, snappy cocktail—the perfect after-dinner drink when you want the night to keep going til the wee hours—is the grown-up sister of the Grasshopper, that creamy-rich dessert in a glass that's stirred up from equal parts crème de menthe, crème de cacao, and cream. Keep your Stinger classy by using a good-quality white crème de menthe, not bottom-shelf stuff that's been dyed shamrock-green.

Like its cousin, the Julep (page 37), the minty flavor and high alcohol content make this a sipping drink, better appreciated when diluted by crushed ice. For a less minty, more potent drink, use 2 ounces brandy and ½ ounce crème de menthe.

2 ounces brandy

1 ounce crème de menthe

Fresh mint sprig, for garnish (optional)

Fill an old fashioned glass with crushed ice. Add brandy and crème de menthe. Stir well. Shake in a glass. Garnish with mint, if desired.

Makes 1 drink

POST-
Prohibition
To
MiD-Century
MODERN

Around the World
in a Glass

When Prohibition was repealed in 1933, it took a little time for a new, public cocktail culture to re-establish itself. Many of the era's popular cocktails came from an expatriate American bartender, Harry Craddock, who fled the States once Prohibition came into effect. He landed in London and became the head barman for the swank Savoy Hotel. Both raffish and elegant, *The Savoy Cocktail Book* he penned helped bring cocktail-hour glamour back across the pond with drinks like the De Rigueur (later popularized in Hollywood as the Brown Derby), the Hoop La, and the White Lady.

As automobile and airplane travel became more commonplace, so did the cocktail hour reach newly cosmopolitan heights, influenced by tastes from around the world. British officers stationed in Burma toasted with rounds of Pegu Clubs, named for an officers' club outside Rangoon. Working at the model rubber plantations set up by car magnate Henry Ford in Brazil, Americans came home with a taste not just for samba but for the Caipirinha, a lime-drenched refresher made with cachaça, the locals' fiery sugarcane spirit. A fad for all things Polynesian was fueled by the tropical island rum drinks popularized by the original Pacific Coast tiki bars, Trader Vic's and Don the Beachcomber.

But few cocktail aficionados could predict what was looming ahead: the overwhelming popularity of a spirit previously known only in ethnic Russian and Polish enclaves. Regardless of Cold War misgivings, the allure of a clear, odorless, high-proof, and mostly tasteless alcohol, easily mixed and hard to detect, would revolutionize our cocktail culture. Those in the know explored this new intoxicant in the Moscow Mule and the James Bond's Vesper Martini. Its name? The Russian word for little water, *vodka*.

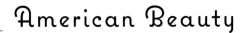

American Beauty

Those long-stemmed red roses carried by every tiara-wearing beauty queen as she weeps, joyfully, down the runway? Most likely they're American Beauty roses, the country's best-selling rose for decades.

The American Beauty cocktail, a 1950s invention, uses grenadine and a float of port to duplicate its namesake's ruby petals. Should your Beauty need a little sweetening, add a few drops of simple syrup (page 7). Just don't use green crème de menthe, which would muddy the color.

¾ ounce brandy

¾ ounce dry vermouth

¾ ounce freshly squeezed orange juice

2 teaspoons grenadine

Dash of white crème de menthe

½ ounce ruby port

Red rose petals, for garnish

Combine brandy, vermouth, orange juice, grenadine, and crème de menthe in a shaker with ice. Shake well. Strain into a chilled cocktail glass. Float the port on top. Garnish with a rose petal or two.

Makes 1 drink

Caipirinha

This Brazilian cocktail is made with cachaça (ka-sha-sa), a potent local spirit distilled from fresh sugarcane. It caught on Stateside during the South American rubber boom in the 1920s and 1930s, when American companies were making fortunes tapping Brazilian rubber trees for the latex sap used to make rubber tires.

Pronounced koo-per-REEN-ya, the caipirinha is made using whole muddled lime sections, which adds the lime peel's fragrant oils to the drink as well as the fruit's tart juice. If you can find it, look for aged cachaça, which is still fiery but a little more smooth, thanks to time spent in French oak barrels.

1 lime, quartered

¼ ounce simple syrup (page 7)

2 ounces cachaça

Put lime quarters, pulp side up, in the bottom of a chilled old fashioned glass. Drizzle simple syrup over lime. Muddle syrup and lime together. Add cachaça. Stir. Fill glass with ice and stir again before serving.

Makes 1 drink

De Rigueur

Grapefruit juice, honey, and whiskey: why, it's practically a health drink! On American shores, this combination, made with bourbon, was known as a Brown Derby, named after Hollywood's famous restaurant, founded in 1929 and reknowned for its down-home food and celebrity clientele.

Across the pond, as recorded in *The Savoy Cocktail Book*, the drink was made with Scotch and more Frenchily known as the De Rigueur—something one just has to have. Pink grapefruit juice gives it a pretty, peachy tint that matches up well with the honey's floral perfume.

1½ ounces Scotch whisky

¾ ounce freshly squeezed pink grapefruit juice

1 teaspoon honey or 2 teaspoons honey syrup (page 56)

Thin quarter-slice of grapefruit, for garnish

Combine ingredients in a shaker with crushed ice. Shake well. Strain into a chilled cocktail glass. Float grapefruit slice on top.

Makes 1 drink

Elephants Sometimes Forget

This fanciful, cherry-laced gin sour comes courtesy of bon vivant Crosby Gaige (1882–1949), author of *Crosby Gaige's Cocktail Guide and Ladies' Companion.* First published in 1941, Gaige's book was less a bartender's manual than a witty, eccentric guide to alcohol-fueled gracious living, written by a man who was both Broadway producer and society host. Gaige liked his prose purple, his companions amusing, his cigarette holders long, and his drinks far from boring.

So slip on the peacock-patterned silk dressing gown and velvet slippers, polish up the bons mots, and raise a toast to the fabulous life.

1 ounce gin

¾ ounce cherry brandy, such as Cherry Heering

¾ ounce freshly squeezed lemon juice

¼ ounce dry vermouth

Dash of orange bitters

A few drops of amaretto (optional)

Long twist of lemon peel, for garnish

Combine gin, cherry brandy, lemon juice, vermouth, and bitters in a shaker with ice. Shake well. Strain into a chilled cocktail glass. Top with a few drops of amaretto, if desired. Garnish with lemon twist.

Makes 1 drink

Hoop La

Named for a British ring-toss game popular at fairgrounds, the Hoop La traces its pedigree to the classic 1930 *The Savoy Cocktail Book*, written by Harry Craddock. As the head mixologist of the Savoy's American Bar, the American-born Craddock livened up the hotel's posh clientele with his brash Stateside concoctions.

Similar to a Sidecar, the Hoop La has one notable addition: Lillet Blanc, a French aperitif made in Bordeaux from white wine fortified with herbs, orange liqueur, and quinine. Originally known as Kina Lillet, its sleek, sexy advertising campaigns were splashed all throughout Europe during the 1920s and 1930s, making it one of the most popular of European aperitifs. Alas, the formula was changed in 1985 to reduce the quinine-based bitterness. Vintage-cocktail fans swear by the Italian Cocchi Aperitivo Americano as the closest match to Kina Lillet.

¾ ounce brandy

¾ ounce Cointreau

¾ ounce Lillet Blanc or Cocchi Aperitivo Americano

¾ ounce freshly squeezed lemon juice

Twist of lemon peel, for garnish

Combine ingredients in a shaker with ice. Shake well. Double strain into a chilled cocktail glass. Garnish with lemon twist.

Makes 1 drink

Mai Tai

Inspired by a trip to Don the Beachcomber, Southern California's first South Seas–themed bar, Victor Bergeron gave his own Oakland bar a tiki makeover in 1937. The result? Trader Vic's, whose instant popularity spawned a craze for Polynesian-style drinks, food, and décor, the more ersatz (pupu platter, anyone?) the better.

The Mai Tai was Bergeron's own creation, whipped up in 1944 for some visiting Tahitian friends and using a well-aged golden Jamaican rum. Orgeat, a fragrant almond syrup typically used to make Italian sodas or flavored coffees, is the Mai Tai's secret ingredient.

2 ounces Jamaican dark rum

½ ounce curaçao

½ ounce freshly squeezed lime juice

Splash of simple syrup (page 7), or to taste

Splash of orgeat (page 7)

Float of rum (optional)

Paper parasol, lime slice, and/or orchid blossom, for garnish

Combine rum, curaçao, lime juice, simple syrup, and orgeat in a shaker with cracked ice. Strain into a tall chilled goblet filled with ice. Float ½ ounce dark rum on top, if desired. Garnish with paper parasol, lime wheel, and/or orchid blossom.

Makes 1 drink

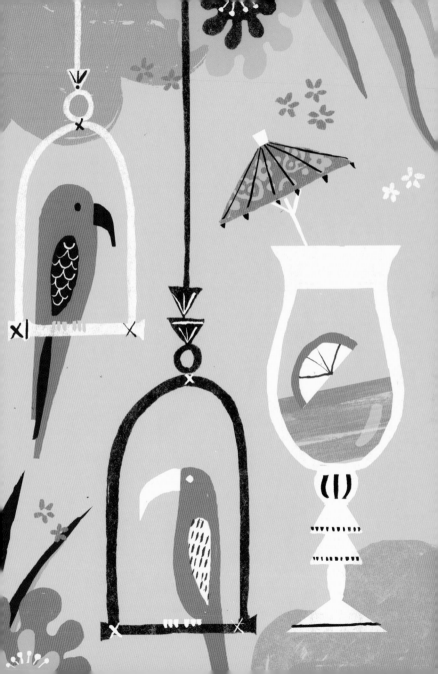

Millionaire

"Who wants to be a millionaire? I don't!" sang Frank Sinatra in the film *High Society*. Clearly, Old Blue Eyes didn't believe his own line, and who would if this luxurious, sunset-hued cocktail came with the loot?

Make this cocktail your excuse for tracking down a gorgeous, burgundy-colored bottle of imported Plymouth sloe gin. Sloes are the bitter, blue-black fruit of the blackthorn bush, and when infused with gin, they make a richly flavored, fruity winter tipple *par excellence*, perfect for sipping by the fire or for spiking mulled wine. Don't even consider substituting a cheap, cough-syrupy American imitation.

¾ ounce Plymouth sloe gin

1½ ounces Jamaican dark rum

¾ ounce apricot brandy

Juice of 1 lime

Combine gin, rum, apricot brandy, and lime juice in a shaker with ice. Shake well. Strain into a chilled cocktail glass.

Makes 1 drink

Moscow Mule

The Moscow Mule was a publicity stunt, born of the felicitous meeting of a Smirnoff vodka salesman, stuck with an unknown Russian product at the beginning of the Cold War, and the down-on-his-luck owner of a Hollywood restaurant, the Cock 'N Bull, who was trying to offload an overstock of ginger beer. Add in some mule-embossed copper mugs, a snappy name, and a marketing coup was born: the Moscow Mule, spicy ginger beer with a hidden vodka kick.

Note that the Mule must be made with British- or Jamaican-style ginger beer; sweet American ginger ale lacks the gingery punch that gets this Mule going.

2 ounces vodka, chilled

Juice of ½ lime

4 ounces ginger beer

Lime wedge, for garnish

Stir vodka and lime juice together in a chilled highball glass or beer mug. Add ice and top with ginger beer. Garnish with lime wedge.

Makes 1 drink

Paloma

Why was this Mexican cocktail dubbed the dove? Maybe because this tall, tart, icy refresher (a long version of the margarita) helps keep the peace, cooling tempers and mellowing moods even as temperatures rise and humidity soars. And the pinch of salt in the drink helps replenish what you've been sweating out through the dog days of August.

In Mexico, Palomas are usually made with grapefruit soda for a drink that's sweet, tart, and just a little bit bitter. To do it this way, replace the fresh grapefruit juice and soda water with a Mexican grapefruit soda. Look for the Jarritos brand in grocery stores specializing in Latin American products.

2 ounces tequila (silver or reposado)
Juice of ½ lime, or to taste
Generous pinch of salt
3 ounces freshly squeezed grapefruit juice
3 ounces soda water
Lime wedge, for garnish

In a tall glass, stir together tequila, lime juice, and salt. Fill the glass with ice and add grapefruit juice and soda. Stir again. Garnish with lime wedge.

Makes 1 drink

Pegu Club

The original Pegu Club was a British officers' club just outside what was then known as Rangoon, the capital of Burma. The club's house drink jazzed up the pink gin (a British Navy staple, made from gin and bitters) with a bracing blast of citrus. Expats and Army men made it a popular tipple in London during the 1920s and 30s, but when Burma went from British colony to independent nation in 1948, the Pegu Club and its cocktail sank into obscurity.

Thank New York City bartender Audrey Saunders for its recent revival. In 2005, she dubbed her new gin-focused bar the Pegu Club and sang the praises of what she called a "crisp, refreshing, and sophisticated" drink.

2 ounces gin

½ ounce orange curaçao

½ ounce freshly squeezed lime juice

Dash of Angostura bitters

Dash of orange bitters

Twist of lime peel, for garnish

Combine ingredients in a shaker with cracked ice. Shake well. Strain into a chilled cocktail glass. Garnish with lime twist.

Makes 1 drink

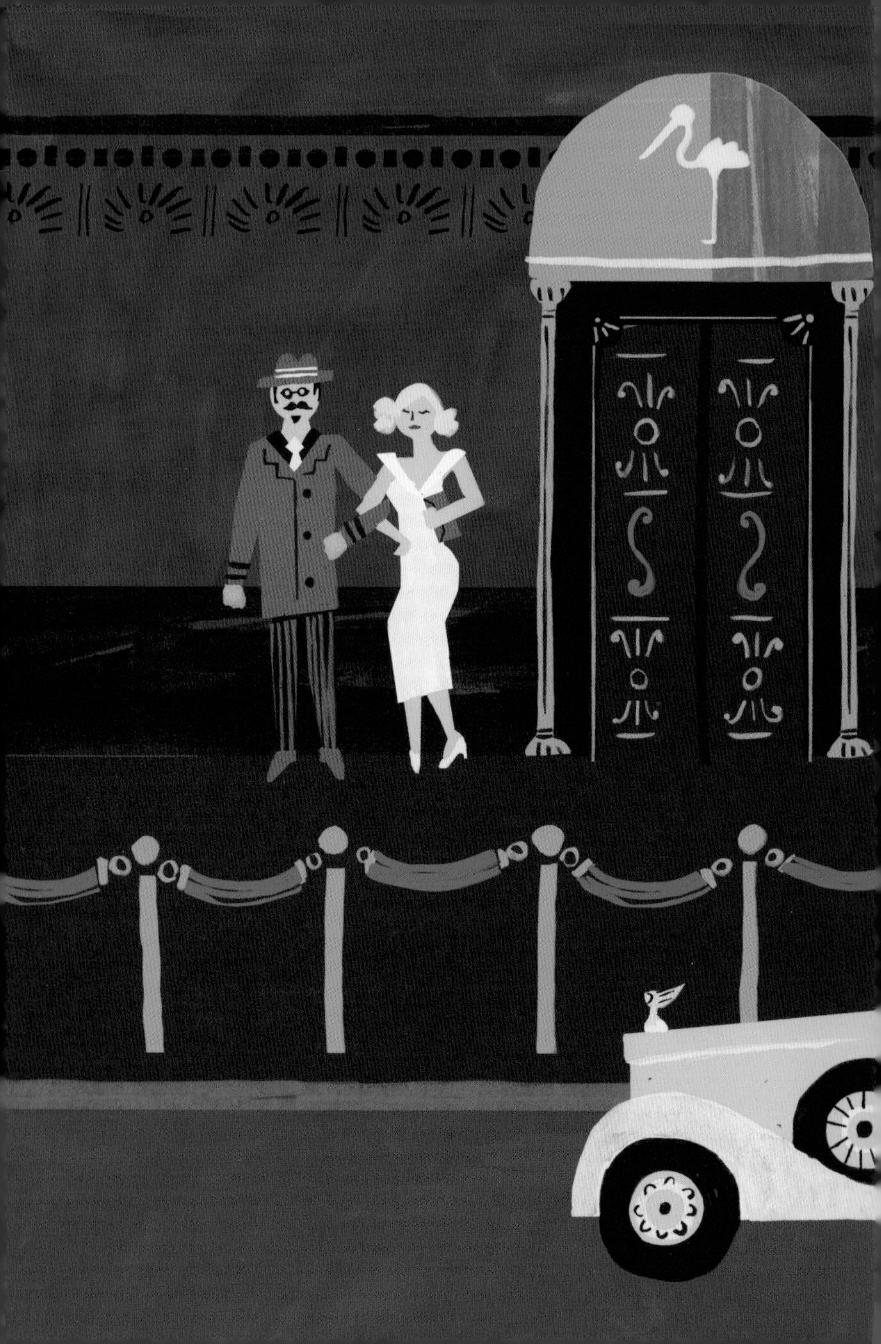

Stork Club

From 1929 to 1965, the Stork Club was New York City's nightclub of choice. The gold chain out front was lifted for society beauties, actors and actresses from Broadway and Hollywood, writers, gossip columnists, prizefighters, politicians, dapper men about town, and debonair officers.

The crème de la crème were always seated at Table 50 in the Cub Room, where bold-face names clinked glasses of the house cocktail, a citrusy blend of gin, Cointreau, and orange and lime juices. This updated version calls for tangerine instead of orange juice, which complements the Cointreau even better.

1½ ounces gin

¾ ounce Cointreau

1 ounce freshly squeezed tangerine juice

½ ounce freshly squeezed lime juice

Dash of orange bitters

Lime slice, for garnish

Combine ingredients in a shaker with cracked ice. Shake well. Strain into a chilled cocktail glass. Garnish with lime slice.

Makes 1 drink

I never have more than one drink before dinner BUT I DO LIKE THAT ONE TO BE **LARGE** AND VERY STRONG *AND* **VERY COLD** and VERY WELL MADE

—JAMES BOND, *CASINO ROYALE*

Vesper Martini

The Vesper Martini was first shaken up at the bar of the Duke's Hotel in London, a favorite hangout of writer Ian Fleming. But it didn't gain international fame until Fleming made it the preferred before-dinner drink of his 007 agent, James Bond. Says Bond, after giving his precise recipe to a bartender in Fleming's first book, *Casino Royale* (1952), "I never have more than one drink before dinner. But I do like that one to be large and very strong and very cold, and very well-made."

Although it's our habit to stir drinks made only with spirits, to be true to Mr. Bond, this drink could, of course, be shaken, not stirred.

2 ounces gin

1 ounce vodka

½ ounce Lillet Blanc or Cocchi Aperitivo Americano

Lemon peel, for garnish

Combine ingredients in a mixing glass with ice. Stir well. Strain into a chilled martini glass. Garnish with lemon twist.

Makes 1 drink

White Lady

This is a Jean Harlowe of a drink, all platinum hair and moonlight shimmering across a bias-cut white satin dress. As in the Ramos Gin Fizz (page 42), a soupçon of fresh egg white gives this cocktail a gliding, ineffable smoothness. But even without the egg white, it remains a lovely drink, elegant and feminine without being pink or girlish. If you prefer to go eggless, a dash of gum syrup can give something of the same thickening effect, plus a little sweetness.

British wine and spirits writer Victoria Moore attributes the White Lady to bartender Harry MacElhone of Harry's at the Ritz in Paris, and claims it as a favorite libation of the swashbuckling Errol Flynn.

2 ounces gin

1 ounce Cointreau

1 ounce freshly squeezed lemon juice

1 teaspoon egg white (optional)

Combine ingredients in a shaker and shake well. Add a generous handful of ice cubes and shake again vigorously. Strain into a chilled cocktail or martini glass.

Makes 1 drink

INDEX